Wine Time!

COLORING BOOK

Jo Taylor

DOVER PUBLICATIONS, INC.
MINEOLA, NEW YORK

Wine is always a good idea! Wine a little, laugh a lot! These are just a couple of the sayings that you'll find in this collection of 31 delightful designs that will put you in the mood for coloring (and perhaps for a glass of wine!). Each expression about wine is placed on a beautifully rendered background that will encourage you to "uncork and unwind," whether you do it on your own or with a group of friends. The illustrations in this book are printed on one side only and are perforated for easy removal and display.

Bibliographical Note

Wine Time! Coloring Book is a new work, first published
by Dover Publications, Inc., in 2018.

International Standard Book Number

ISBN-13: 978-0-486-82754-4
ISBN-10: 0-486-82754-2

Manufactured in the United States by LSC Communications
82754202   2019
www.doverpublications.com

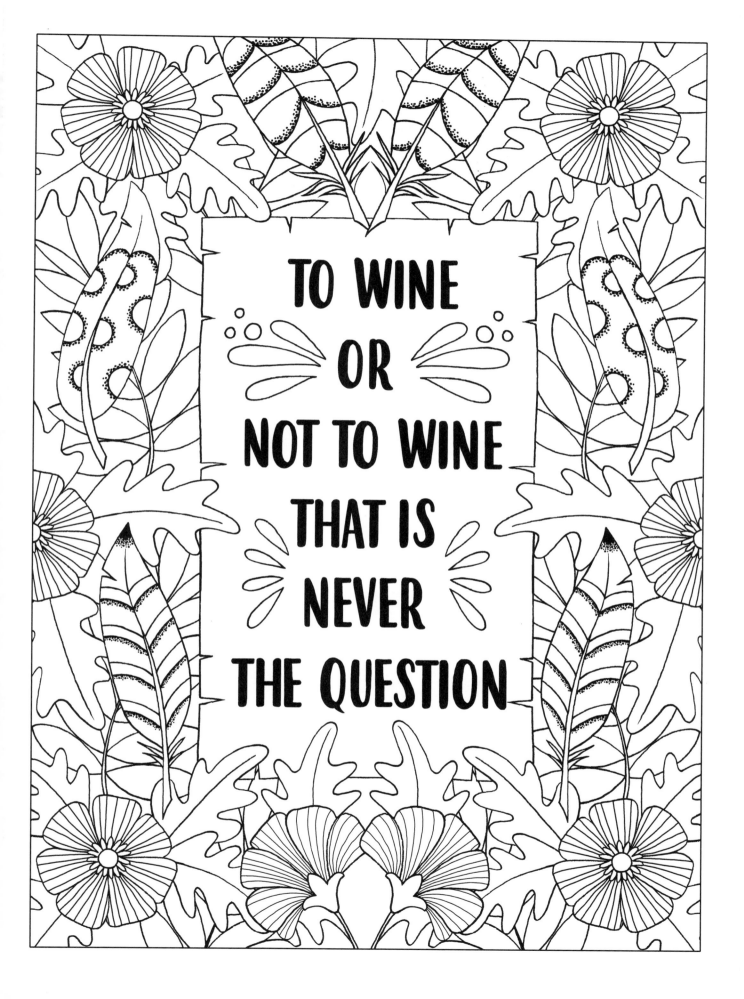

TO WINE
OR
NOT TO WINE
THAT IS
NEVER
THE QUESTION

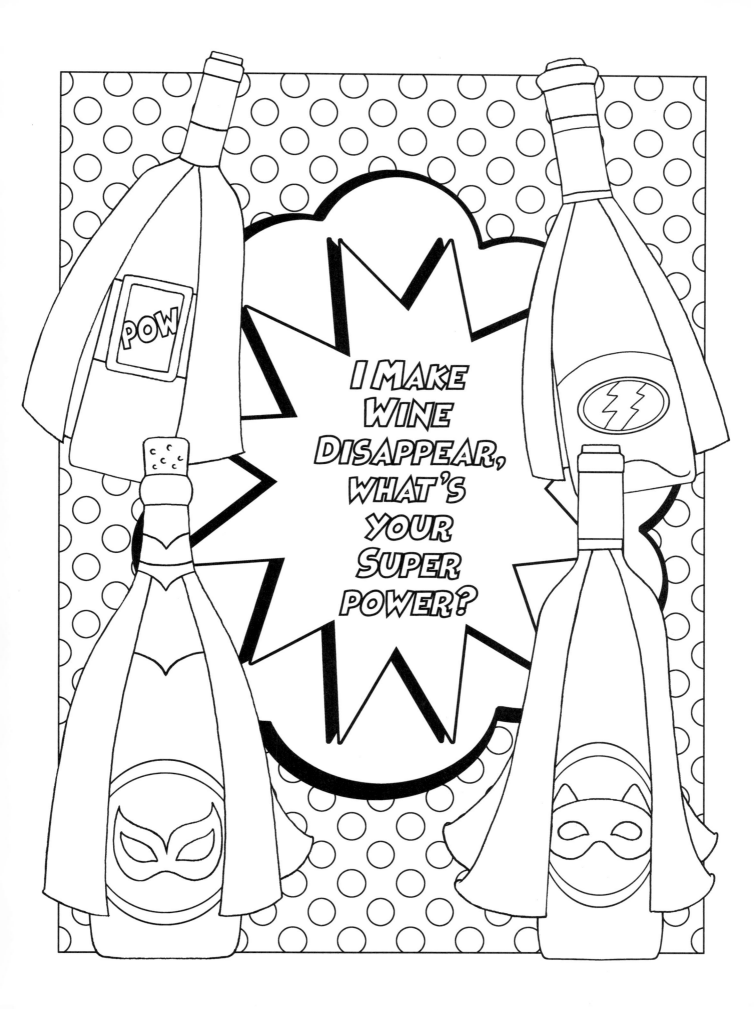

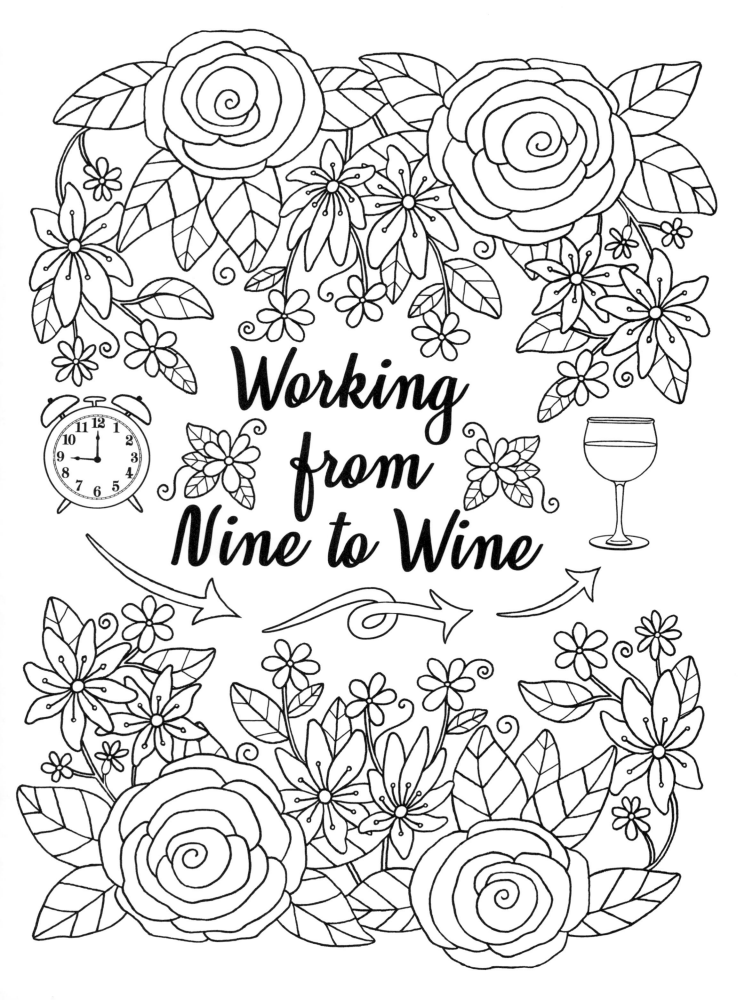

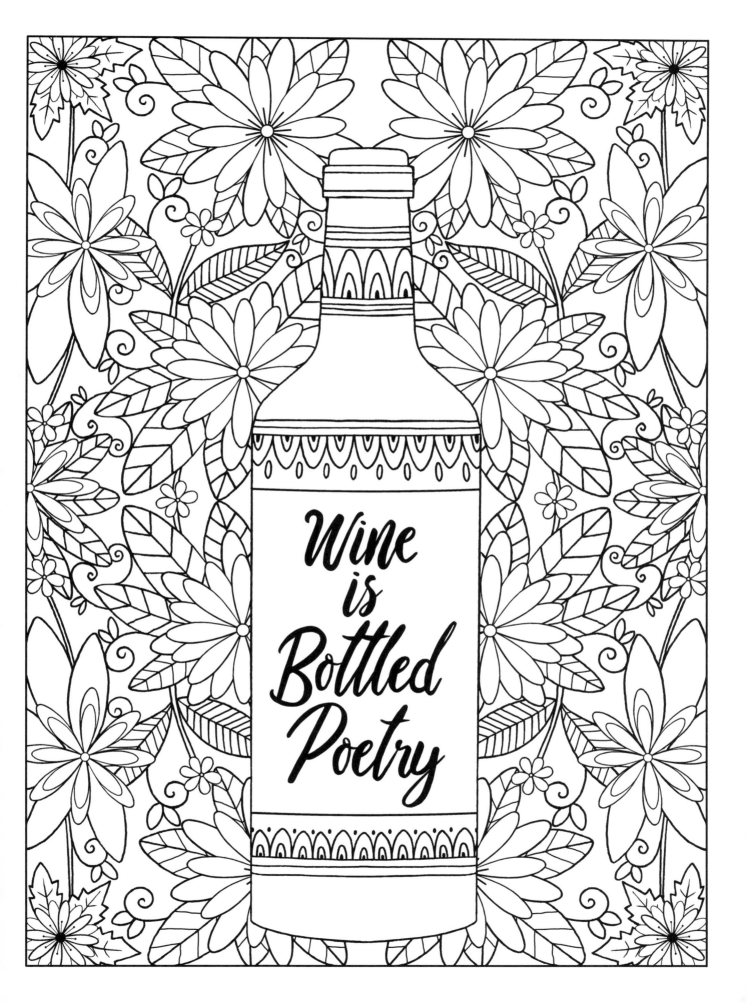

True friends don't care if your house is messy. They care if you have wine.